The red man and the green man live inside the traffic lights.

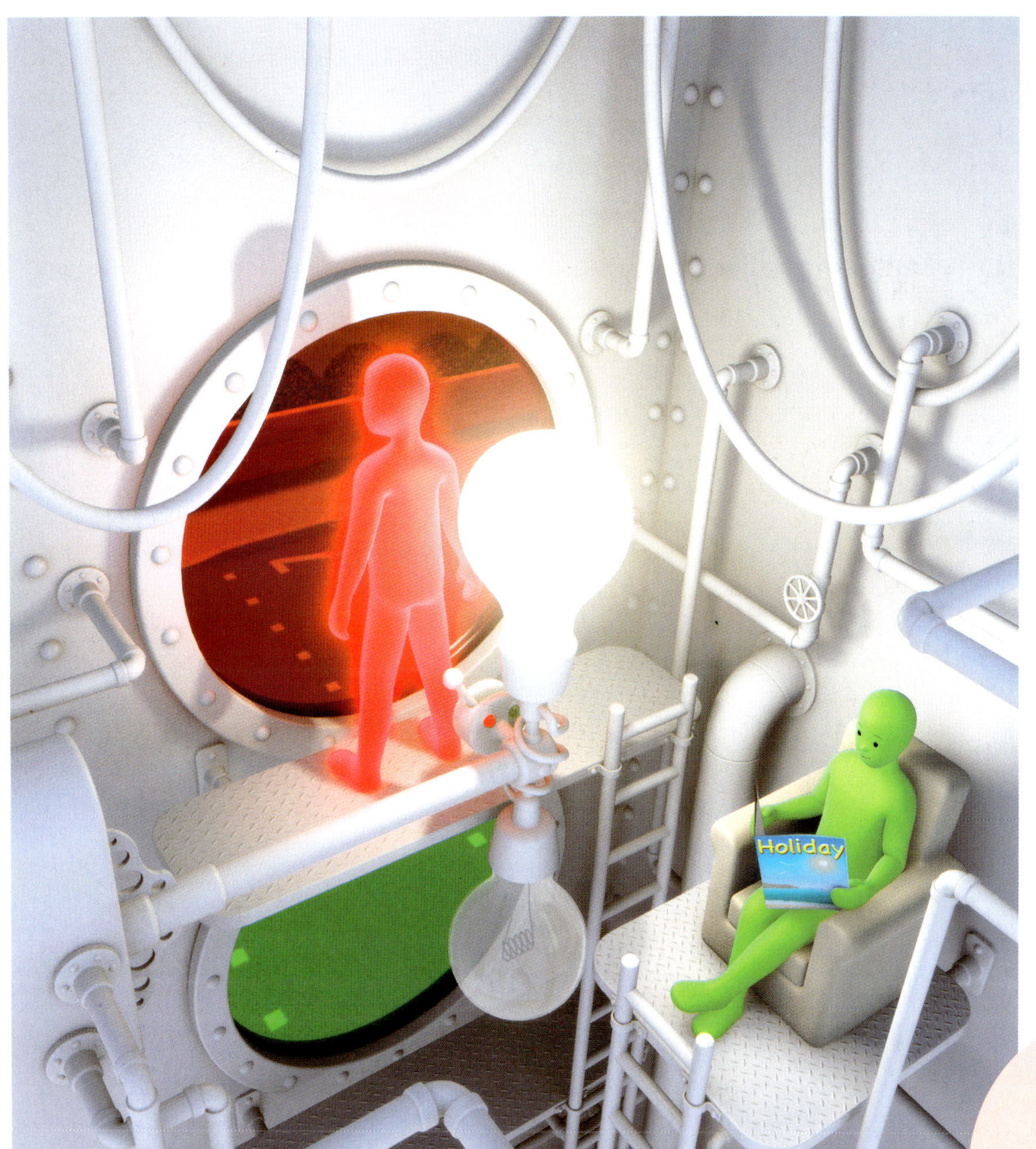

When people see the red man, they stop. When people see the green man, they can cross the road.

"I'm sick of these traffic lights," the red man says one day.
"So am I," says the green man.
"Let's go on holiday."

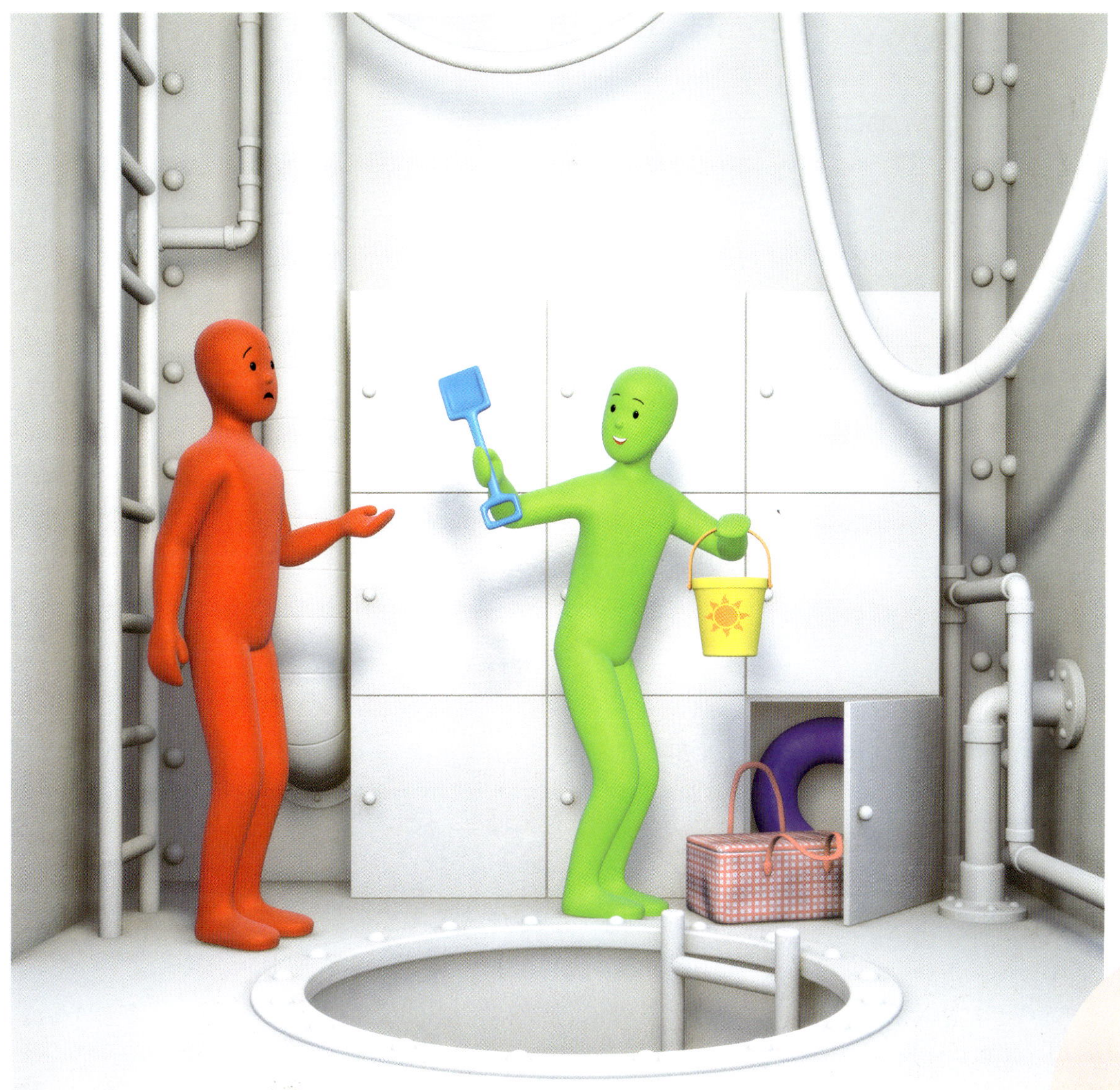

The red man and the green man get on a train. "Go, train, go," says the green man. But the train stays still.

In the end the train goes. The red man and the green man have a cup of tea.

The red man sees the sea. "Stop, train, stop!" he cries. But the train keeps going.

In the end the train stops. The red man and the green man get off.

The two men go to the beach. They make some traffic lights in the sand.

But then the waves roll in.
"Stop, waves, stop!" cries the red man. But the waves don't stop.

They see a sea snail. It is sitting on a rock.

"Go, snail, go!" says the green man. But the snail stays still.

"No one stops when I tell them," says the red man. "And no one goes when I tell them," says the green man. "Let's go home."

The red man and the green man go back on the train.

Back home, no one knows when to cross the road. They are happy to see the red man and the green man again.

The two men hop up into the traffic lights.

"The seaside is all right, but here people do what we tell them," they say.

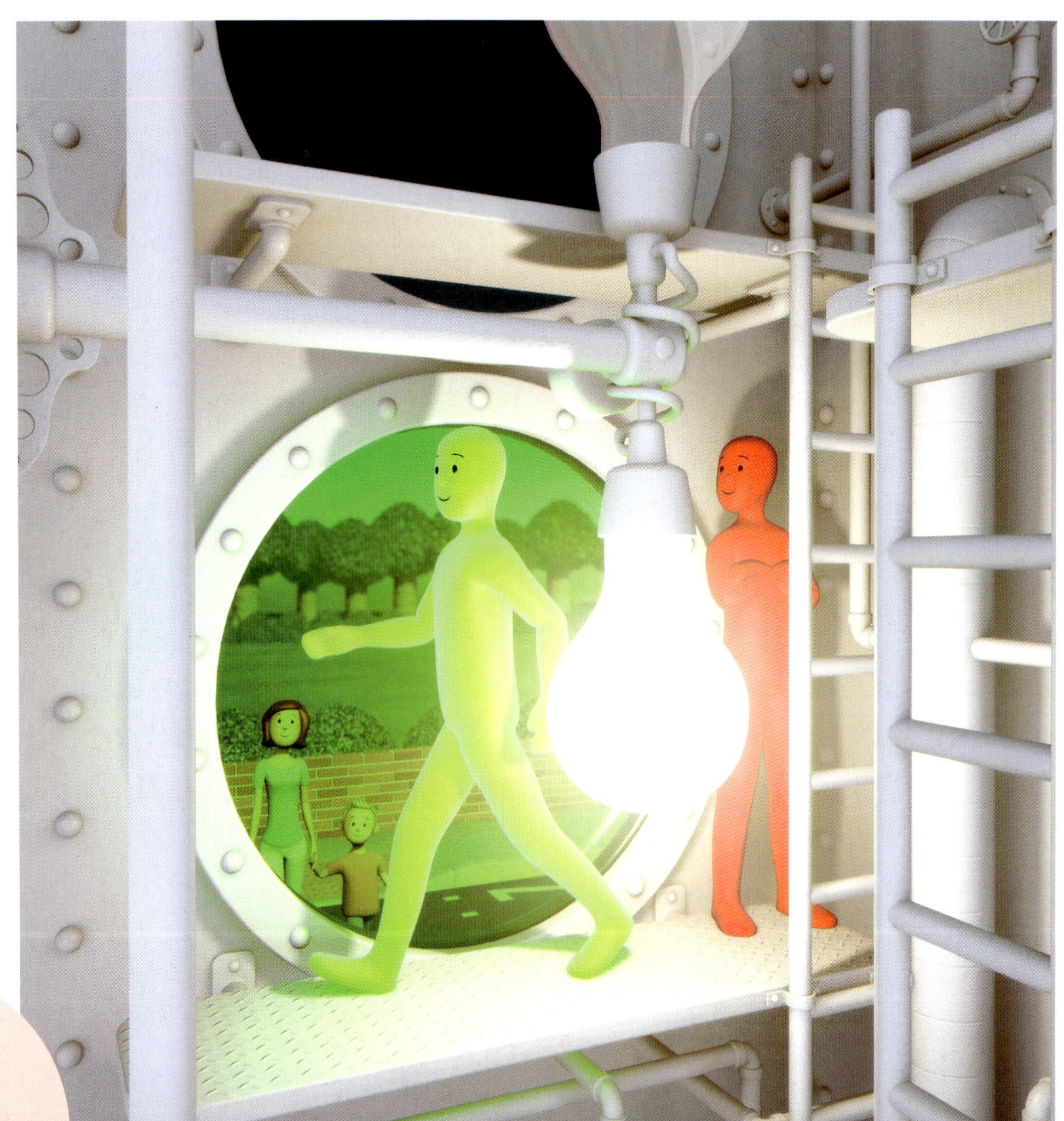